Web Workers

Ido Green

O'REILLY®

Beijing · Cambridge · Farnham · Köln · Sebastopol · Tokyo

Web Workers

by Ido Green

Published by O'Reilly Media, Inc., 1005 Gravenstein Highway North, Sebastopol, CA 95472.

O'Reilly books may be purchased for educational, business, or sales promotional use. Online editions are also available for most titles (*http://my.safaribooksonline.com*). For more information, contact our corporate/institutional sales department: 800-998-9938 or *corporate@oreilly.com*.

Editors: Mike Loukides and Simon St. Laurent
Production Editor: Dan Fauxsmith
Proofreader: O'Reilly Media Publishing Services

Cover Designer: Karen Montgomery
Interior Designer: David Futato
Illustrator: Robert Romano

Revision History for the First Edition:

2012-05-22   First release

See *http://oreilly.com/catalog/errata.csp?isbn=9781449322137* for release details.

ISBN: 978-1-449-32213-7

[LSI]

1337631787

To Ema
Who always multi threaded

Table of Contents

Preface vii

1. Overview 1
   What Can Web Workers Do?   2
   Creating a Worker   3
   What Web Workers Can and Can't Do   3
   Worker Execution   4
   Web Workers API Browser Availability   4

2. How and Where Can We Use Web Workers? 7
   Loading External Scripts   9

3. Dedicated Workers 13
   Control Your Web Workers   17
   Parsing Data with Workers   21
   Transferable Objects   21

4. Inline Workers 23

5. Shared Workers 29

6. Debug Your Workers 39
   Debugging in Chrome Dev Tools   40

7. Web Workers Beyond the Browser: Node 43
   Processes   43
   Communications   44
   Message Format   45
   Code   45
   API   45
   Additional Resources   46

Preface

Web Workers is a powerful feature of HTML5 that hasn't received very much attention. It provides an API that allows you to run JavaScript in a separate thread that doesn't interfere with the user interface of your web application. This JavaScript runs in parallel with the main renderer and any of your user interface scripts on it. This allows long and "processing-heavy" tasks to be executed without making the page unresponsive.

Like threads in other technologies, Web Workers are relatively heavyweight. You don't want to use them in large numbers, as each one consumes significant system resources. Web Workers are expected to handle long tasks that rely on constrained resources (e.g., CPU, network bandwidth, etc.). They have a high startup cost and a high instance of memory cost.

Because it is a new, evolving standard, different browsers implement the Web Workers specification in different ways. Although some aspects of the implementation are stabilizing, I suspect that features like access to IndexedDB will be available soon in most modern browsers. I hope that with this book and the adoption of modern browsers we will see more usage of this powerful API.

 All the examples in this book were tested on Chrome (15+) and Firefox (7+). Web Workers also work in mobile Safari 5+, and will be especially useful because the new iPhone 4GS has a multi-core processor.

How This Book Is Organized

Before you can do much with Web Workers, it helps to know what they are and what they can do well. Next, you'll learn how to confirm that your browser supports this feature with a simple "Web Worker Hello World" example. The next three chapters cover the different kinds of Web Workers (dedicated, shared, and inline), showing how to use each one of them and when it will be best to choose one over the other. After that, you'll explore best practices for debugging your Web Workers. Finally, because Web Workers are also used outside of a browser, you'll see how to apply them within the server-side Node environment.

Who This Book Is For

You should have a solid intermediate to advanced understanding of JavaScript before tackling the tools used in this book. In particular, you need to understand event handling and callbacks.

Conventions Used in This Book

The following typographical conventions are used in this book:

Italic

> Indicates new terms, URLs, email addresses, filenames, and file extensions.

`Constant width`

> Used for program listings, as well as within paragraphs to refer to program elements such as variable or function names, databases, data types, environment variables, statements, and keywords.

`Constant width bold`

> Shows commands or other text that should be typed literally by the user.

`Constant width italic`

> Shows text that should be replaced with user-supplied values or by values determined by context.

 This icon signifies a tip, suggestion, or general note.

 This icon indicates a warning or caution.

Using Code Examples

This book is here to help you get your job done. In general, you may use the code in this book in your programs and documentation. You do not need to contact us for permission unless you're reproducing a significant portion of the code. For example, writing a program that uses several chunks of code from this book does not require permission. Selling or distributing a CD-ROM of examples from O'Reilly books does require permission. Answering a question by citing this book and quoting example code does not require permission. Incorporating a significant amount of example code from this book into your product's documentation does require permission.

We appreciate, but do not require, attribution. An attribution usually includes the title, author, publisher, and ISBN. For example: "*Web Workers* by Ido Green (O'Reilly). Copyright 2012 Ido Green, 9781449322137."

If you feel your use of code examples falls outside fair use or the permission given above, feel free to contact us at *permissions@oreilly.com*.

Safari® Books Online

 Safari Books Online (*www.safaribooksonline.com*) is an on-demand digital library that delivers expert content in both book and video form from the world's leading authors in technology and business.

Technology professionals, software developers, web designers, and business and creative professionals use Safari Books Online as their primary resource for research, problem solving, learning, and certification training.

Safari Books Online offers a range of product mixes and pricing programs for organizations, government agencies, and individuals. Subscribers have access to thousands of books, training videos, and prepublication manuscripts in one fully searchable database from publishers like O'Reilly Media, Prentice Hall Professional, Addison-Wesley Professional, Microsoft Press, Sams, Que, Peachpit Press, Focal Press, Cisco Press, John Wiley & Sons, Syngress, Morgan Kaufmann, IBM Redbooks, Packt, Adobe Press, FT Press, Apress, Manning, New Riders, McGraw-Hill, Jones & Bartlett, Course Technology, and dozens more. For more information about Safari Books Online, please visit us online.

How to Contact Us

Please address comments and questions concerning this book to the publisher:

O'Reilly Media, Inc.
1005 Gravenstein Highway North
Sebastopol, CA 95472
800-998-9938 (in the United States or Canada)
707-829-0515 (international or local)
707-829-0104 (fax)

We have a web page for this book, where we list errata, examples, and any additional information. You can access this page at:

http://oreil.ly/webworkers-1e

To comment or ask technical questions about this book, send email to:

bookquestions@oreilly.com

For more information about our books, courses, conferences, and news, see our website at *http://www.oreilly.com*.

Find us on Facebook: *http://facebook.com/oreilly*

Follow us on Twitter: *http://twitter.com/oreillymedia*

Watch us on YouTube: *http://www.youtube.com/oreillymedia*

Acknowledgments

I would like to thank Eric Bidelman for doing great review job. Without him, most of the examples would have crashed after 10 seconds.

CHAPTER 1

Overview

Modern web applications would often run better if there was a way to perform heavy calculations in the background instead of making the user interface wait for them to complete. The Web Workers specification[1] defines an API for running computationally intensive code in a thread other than the web application user interface. Long tasks can run without affecting your interface's memory and CPU footprint because the Worker will live in its own thread.

Multi-threaded programing is a complicated subject well stocked with complex algorithms and theoretical discussion. You can find other languages (e.g., Java) that give their developers a library to mask some of the complexity[2]. The good news is that Web Workers provides a nice and *simple* API that lets you be very productive without worrying too much about deadlocks and similar problems.

Web Workers promises to end the unfriendly "unresponsive script" dialogs like the ones shown in Figure 1-1 and Figure 1-2.

Figure 1-1. The warning dialog for "unresponsive script" in Windows

---

1. *http://www.whatwg.org/specs/web-apps/current-work/multipage/workers.html*

2. *http://gee.cs.oswego.edu/dl/concurrency-interest/index.html* - and for more about multi-threading *http://en .wikipedia.org/wiki/Multithreading_(computer_architecture)* is a good place to start your exploration.

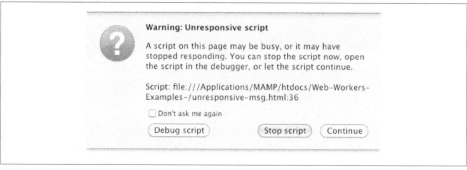

Figure 1-2. The warning dialog for "unresponsive script" in MacOS

What Can Web Workers Do?

If your web application needs to complete a task that takes more than 150 milliseconds, you should consider using a Web Worker. If your app needs to feel like a native one, you should even consider setting the bar at around 80 milliseconds. Timing, of course, depends on your browser and hardware. If you are building a mobile web application you should make this time even shorter, as the CPU is not as powerful as on your desktop.[3] Before you get into timing your specific application, though, you may want to contemplate tasks like the following:

- Encoding/decoding a large string
- Complex mathematical calculations (e.g., prime numbers, encryption, simulated annealing, etc.)
- Sorting a large array
- Network requests and resulting data processing
- Calculations and data manipulation on local storage
- Prefetching and/or caching data
- Code syntax highlighting or other real-time text analysis (e.g., spell checking)
- Image manipulation
- Analyzing or processing video or audio data (including face and voice recognition)
- Background I/O
- Polling web services
- Processing large arrays or huge JSON responses

---

3. Web Workers in mobile browsers - *http://greenido.wordpress.com/2012/02/07/google-chrome-for-android-is-out-there/*

Creating a Worker

To create a new Worker using the Web Worker API, you just need to call its script. For example:

```
var worker = new Worker("worker.js");
```

The above line will load the script located at "worker.js" and execute it in the background. You need to call the `Worker()` constructor with the URI of a script to execute in the Worker thread. If you want to get data from the Worker (e.g., output of processed information, notifications, etc.), you should set the Worker's `onmessage` property to an appropriate event handler function. For example:

```
var worker = new Worker('routes.js');
worker.onmessage = function(event) {
  console.log("Called back by the routes-worker with the best route to the pub");
}
```

You can also keep in touch with your Workers using `addEventListener`:

```
var worker = new Worker('routes.js');
worker.addEventListener('message', function(event) {
  console.log("Called back by the routes-worker... with the best route to the pub")
}, false);
worker.postMessage(); // start the worker.
```

What Web Workers Can and Can't Do

Workers don't have access to the DOM of the "parent" page. They can't access any of the following:

* The `window` object
* The `document` object
* The `parent` object
* And, last but not least, they can't use JavaScript libraries that depend on these objects to work, like jQuery.

Web Workers can access only a limited set of JavaScript's features because of their multi-threaded nature. Here is the set of features they can use:

* The `navigator` object
* The `location` object (read-only)
* The `XMLHttpRequest` function
* The `atob()` and `btoa()` functions for converting Base 64 ASCII to and from binary data
* `setTimeout()` / `clearTimeout()` and `setInterval()` / `clearInterval()`
* `dump()`

- The application cache
- External scripts using the `importScripts()` method
- Spawning other Web Workers[4]

Worker Execution

Web Workers threads run their code synchronously from top to bottom, and then enter an asynchronous phase in which they respond to events and timers. This allows roughly two types of Web Workers:

- Web Workers that register an `onmessage` event handler, for long-running tasks that need to run in the background. This Web Worker won't exit, as it keeps listening for new messages.
- Web Workers that never register for `onmessage` events, handling single tasks that need to be offset from the main web app thread, like fetching and parsing a massive JSON object. This Web Worker will exit once the operation is over. (In some cases, where you have registered callbacks, it will wait until all of the callbacks are done.)

Web Workers API Browser Availability

Table 1-1 shows that most modern browsers implement basic Web Workers. Even the mobile browsers offer Web Workers. However, Table 1-2 shows less support for the shared Web Workers, which are covered in Chapter 5.

Table 1-1. Web Worker support in various browsers

Browser	Version
IE	10.0
Chrome	12+
Firefox	5+
Safari	4+
Opera	11+
iOS Safari	5+
Opera Mobile	11+
Android	2.1
Chrome for Android	Beta

---

4. *http://www.html5rocks.com/en/tutorials/workers/basics/#toc-enviornment-subworkers*

Table 1-2. Shared Web Worker support in various browsers

Browser	Version
IE	Support unknown for 10.0
Chrome	12+
Firefox	Support unknown for 9+
Safari	5+
Opera	11+
iOS Safari	5+
Opera Mobile	11+

CHAPTER 2

How and Where Can We Use Web Workers?

When we wish to use a feature that is not supported in all browsers, we need to check for support. In our case, for Web Workers we need to check whether there is a `Worker` property on the global window object. If the browser does not support the Web Worker API, the Worker property will be undefined, and you will need to find another approach. (Hopefully you designed your application on a progressive enhancement model, and this won't be fatal.) We can use this simple helper function to sniff for Web Workers support:

```
isWorkersAvailable() {
 return !!window.Worker;
}
```

Instead of using the function above, you could use the Modernizr library (*http://mod ernizr.com*) to detect whether the client's browser supports Web Workers. This would let you test to see whether the client browser supports Web Workers and do something else if it doesn't:

```
if (Modernizr.webworkers) {
 // window.Worker is available!
} else {
 // no native support for Web Workers
}
```

Now that we know that our browser can leverage Web Workers, let's have a look at a simple example that calculates prime numbers, a popular "Hello World" of the Web Workers world, shown in Example 2-1 and Example 2-2. Figure 2-1 shows the results.

Example 2-1. highPrime.js, a brute force prime number calculator that can be used as a Web Worker

```
//
// A simple way to find prime numbers
//
var n = 1;
search: while (true) {
```

```
  n += 1;
  for (var i = 2; i <= Math.sqrt(n); i += 1) {
    if (n % i == 0) {
      continue search;
    }
  }
  // found a prime!
  postMessage(n);
}
```

Example 2-2. An HTML host for the highPrime.js Web Worker

```
<!DOCTYPE HTML>
<html>
<head>
 <title>Web Worker: The highest prime number</title>
</head>
<style>
    #result {
        background-color: yellow;
        padding: 20px;
        font-size: 140%;
    }
    footer {
        font-size: 70%;
        color: red;
        position: fixed;
        bottom: 1em;
        text-align: center;
    }
</style>
<body>

  <h1>Web Worker: The highest prime number</h1>
  <article>The highest prime number discovered so far is:
      <output id="result"></output>
  </article>
  <script>
   var worker = new Worker('highPrime.js');
   worker.onmessage = function (event) {
     document.getElementById('result').textContent = event.data;
   };
  </script>
</body>
</html>
```

 Due to Chrome's security restrictions, Web Workers will not run locally (e.g., from *file://*) in the latest versions of the browser (16+). Instead, they fail silently! To run your app using local files and the *file://* scheme, run Chrome with the `--allow-file-access-from-files` flag set. It is not recommended to run your regular browser with this flag set. It should only be used for testing or development purposes.

In Chrome 17+ you will get "Uncaught Error: SECURITY_ERR: DOM Exception 18", which will be a reminder that you need to run from a local server while developing. You can see how it looks in Figure 2-1.

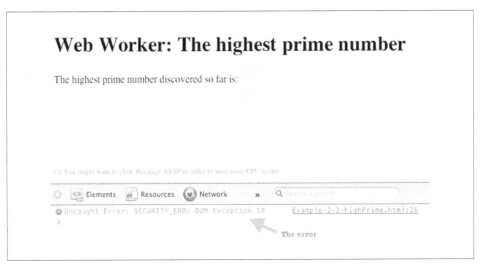

Figure 2-1. Reporting on the prime number–generating Web Worker

Messages sent between our web app page and the Web Worker using `postMessage()` will be copied (not shared). Our main web app page and the Web Worker don't point to the same object instance, so we have a duplicate memory footprint on each end. In modern browsers, this capability is enabled by JSON encoding/decoding the object value on each side (web app page and the worker). This means that you may pass JSON or any other serialized data. For example:

```
postMessage ({'cmd': 'start', 'time': Date.now() });
```

Loading External Scripts

To load external script files or libraries into a Web Worker, use the `importScripts()` global function. This function takes strings as arguments for the resources to import. If you give it zero URLs nothing will be invoked. However, if you give it one or more URLs (and file names as well), then it will load and execute this JavaScript (regardless of the MIME type) in the Web Worker.

This code loads *script1.js* and *script2.js* into a Worker:

```
importScripts('script1.js');
importScripts('script2.js');
```

This can also be written as a single line:

```
importScripts('script1.js', 'script2.js');
```

The browser may fetch the scripts in any order, and in case of failure will return a *NetworkError* exception. After all of the fetching is done, the scripts will be run in the order in which you wrote them as arguments in *importScripts()*. These commands will be processed synchronously. The *importScripts()* function itself does not return until all the scripts have been fetched and executed.

 Web Worker scripts must be resources (URLs of external files) with the same scheme as their calling page. In other words, you won't be able to load a script from a JavaScript URL. Moreover, if your web app is working on a secure HTTP (https) you will need to call the Web Worker on *https://* as well.

There is currently (a tiny) disagreement among browser vendors on whether or not data URIs are of the same origin; Chrome (15+) and Gecko 10.0+ permit data URIs as a valid source for Web Workers.

One way to use `importScripts()` is by passing the script a callback function that will be handling the results from the work that the Web Worker crunches. Example 2-3 demonstrates using a callback function by setting a call to the Twitter API and setting a handling function `processTweets` that will handle the data Twitter returns.

```
importScripts('http://twitter.com/statuses/user_timeline/' +
    user + '.json?count=10&callback=processTweets');
 .
 .
 .
function processTweets(data) {
   // parse the json object that holds the tweets and build a html block from
   // their content.
   .
   .
   .
}
```

Example 2-3. Code that runs from index.html for creating a Web Worker

```
function startWorker(settings) {
 var myWorker = new Worker('scripts/worker.js');
 myWorker.addEventListener("message", workerListener, false);
 myWorker.postMessage(settings);
}
```

Example 2-4. The worker.js file

```
self.addEventListener('message', function(e) {
 doSomeWork();
};

function doSomeWork() {
 importScripts('http://example.com?callBack=handleWorkerResults');
}

function handleWorkerResults() {
 postMessage(result);
}
```

This can be a useful way to fetch JSON from REST APIs and then work on it. The "Fetch Tweet" example in the next chapter demonstrates this technique.

CHAPTER 3

Dedicated Workers

Dedicated Web Workers let you run scripts in background threads. Once the Web Worker is running, it can communicate with its web app by posting messages to an event handler registered with the web app that spawned it. Dedicated Web Workers are good for tasks that consume a lot of CPU (e.g., calculating routes, 3D positions, prime numbers, etc.) and are also good for masking the latency in server connections. Having a Worker handle the connections keeps the main user interface thread freer to handle the users' actions.

A dedicated Web Worker supports two events:

onmessage
> Triggered when a message is received. An event object with a data member will be provided with the message.

onerror
> Triggered when an error occurs in the Worker thread. The event provides a data member with the error information.

In this example, our web application main page starts a Web Worker to pull data from the server. Once it receives the data, the Web Worker sends it to the parent page so it can save it in the client-side database (or in our example, the localStorage). In the real world we can take this methodology one step further and let our Web Worker handle all of the communication with the server.

Example 3-1 does several things:

1. Starts the Web Worker code (which is in Example 3-2) by calling its constructor:
   `var worker = new Worker("Example-3-2-tweet.js");`.
2. Sets itself up to listen for messages (the tweet information) the Web Worker will send, using `worker.addEventListener`.
3. When tweets arrive from the Web Worker, create a new DOM element (list <ul>) and add the list items (<li>) with the text from the tweets. After the loop completes, use one command to update the DOM. This is the better way to make changes to

your web app. Try to avoid refresh/repaint of the DOM in side loops. It's very inefficient, and the browser's life will be easier with fewer DOM changes that contain more data in them.

4. Save the tweets inside the loop using the time stamp of the tweet as our key for the `localStorage`.

 In real life web app scenarios, you should avoid updating the `localStor age` (just like the DOM) inside loops.

Example 3-1. Index.html for fetching tweets and putting them in localStorage

```html
<!DOCTYPE HTML>
<html>
  <head>
    <meta charset="utf-8" />
    <meta http-equiv="X-UA-Compatible" content="IE=edge,chrome=1">
    <title>Web Workers: Pull Tweets and save them in local storage</title>
    <meta name="author" content="Ido Green">
    <script src="http://ajax.googleapis.com/ajax/libs/jquery/1/jquery.min.js"></script>
    <style>
      #result {
        background: lightblue;
        padding: 20px;
        border-radius: 18px;
      }
      #tweets {
        background: yellow;
        border-radius: 28px;
        padding: 20px;
      }
    </style>
  </head>
  <body>

    <h1>Web Workers: Pull Tweets and save them in local storage</h1>
    <article>In this example we used a Web Worker to read tweets and save them using
localStorage.<br/>
      Let's have a look at how it's working internally by opening Chrome Dev Tool on the
'Resources' tab.<br/>
      Then, click on Local Storage and you will see the data of the tweets saved by tweet-
id.<br/>
      For more info: <a href="http://www.w3.org/TR/workers/">www.w3.org/TR/workers</a>
      <br/>
      <div id="result"></div>
      <div id="tweets"></div>
    </article>

    <script>
      console.log("WebWorker: Starting");
      var worker = new Worker("Example-3-2-tweet.js");
      worker.addEventListener("message", function(e) {
```

```
    var curTime = new Date();
    // here we will show the messages between our page and the Worker
    $('#result').append( curTime + " ) " + e.data + "<br/>");
    var source = e.data[0].source;
    // in case we have some data from Twitter - let's show it to the user
    if (typeof source != 'undefined' ) {
      var tweets = document.createElement("ul");
      for (var i=0; i < 10; i++) {
        if (typeof e.data[i] != 'undefined' &&
                  e.data[i].text != 'undefined') {
          var tweetTextItem = document.createElement("li");
          var tweetText = document.createTextNode(e.data[i].text + " | " +
             e.data[i].source  + " (" +
             e.data[i].created_at + ")" ) ;
          tweetTextItem.appendChild(tweetText);
          tweets.appendChild(tweetTextItem);
          saveTweet(e.data[i]);
        }
      }
      // update the DOM outside our loop so it will be efficient
      console.log("WebWorker: Updated the DOM with Tweets");
      $("#tweets").append(tweets);
    }
  }, false);

  worker.onerror = function(e){
    throw new Error(e.message + " (" + e.filename + ":" + e.lineno + ")");
  };

  // Key - tweet ID
  // Val - Time tweet created and the text of the tweet.
  function saveTweet(tweet) {
    localStorage.setItem(tweet.id_str, "{"+
      "'created': '" + tweet.created_at + "'," +
      "'tweet-text': '" + tweet.text + "'}");
  }

  // Get a tweet from our localStorage. We could use sessionStorage if we
  // wish to have this data just for our session
  function getTweet(tweetID) {
    return localStorage.getItem(tweetID);
  }

  </script>
 </body>
</html>
```

The Web Worker itself (Example 3-2) has only two steps. First, it reads tweets from Twitter API inside readTweets(). The callback function executes processT weets(data), which takes the payload JSON and sends it to the parent (e.g., in‐dex.html). It also sends some "administrative" messages like "Worker Status:" so it will be easy to debug the code and see progress. The last phase is a loop that makes sure to call the Twitter API every 3 seconds.

In addition, we can use *app cache* and offline capabilities to handle cases in which we have a weak network connection or no connection at all.

Example 3-2. The Web Worker that collects the tweets

```javascript
// Example-3-2-tweet.js
// Pull Tweets and send them so the parent page could save them in the localStorage
var connections = 0;      // count active connections
var updateDelay = 30000; // = 30sec delay
var user = "greenido";

function getURL(user) {
  return 'http://twitter.com/statuses/user_timeline/' + user
  + '.json?count=' + 12 + '&callback=processTweets';
}

function readTweets() {
  try {
    var url = getURL(user);
    postMessage("Worker Status: Attempting To Read Tweets for user - " + user +
      " from: "+ url);
    importScripts(url);
  }
  catch (e) {
    postMessage("Worker Status: Error - " + e.message);
    setTimeout(readTweets, updateDelay);
  }
}

function processTweets(data) {
  var numTweets = data.length;
  if (numTweets > 0) {
    postMessage("Worker Status: New Tweets - " +  numTweets);
    postMessage(data);
  } else {
    postMessage("Worker Status: New Tweets - 0");
  }
  setTimeout(readTweets, updateDelay);
}

//
// start the party in the Worker
//
readTweets();
```

Figure 3-1 shows how the simple web app looks with the Chrome Dev Tool open:

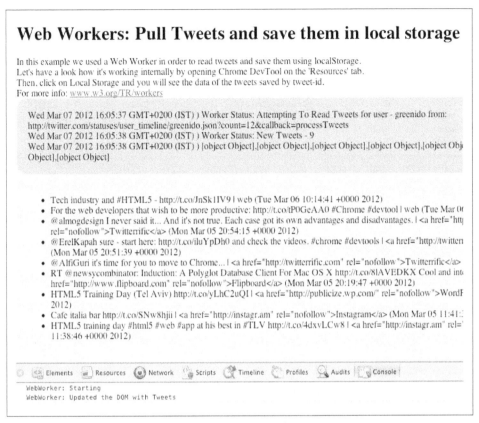

Figure 3-1. *Putting tweets in local storage with a Web Worker*

There are cases in which you wish to gain more control on the operation of the Web Worker. In the next example we will see how to manage a Web Worker with a simple protocol created using a JSON object that contains a command and payload:

```
{'cmd': 'start/stop', 'upto': max number for our prime calculation}
```

Control Your Web Workers

Example 3-3 and Example 3-4 demonstrate managing our prime number–calculating Web Worker with a simple protocol of two commands: *start* and *stop*. You can, of course, have many more commands that suit the specific case you are trying to solve. It's important to remember that in our main `switch` you should always keep a `default` and report it as an error (or warning depending on your app). The results are shown in Figure 3-2.

Example 3-3. HTML file for a more controllable prime number calculator.

```
<!DOCTYPE HTML>
<html>
 <head>
   <title>Web Worker: The highest prime number</title>
   <!-- Get the latest jQuery code -->
   <script src="http://ajax.googleapis.com/ajax/libs/jquery/1/jquery.min.js"></script>
   <meta charset=utf-8 />
 </head>
 <style>
   #actions {
     position: fixed;
     top: 10px;
     background: lightBlue;
     padding:8px;
   }
   h1 {
     position: relative;
     bottom: 10px;
     left: 280px;
   }
   #status {
     position: relative;
     font-size: 120%;
     background: darkslategrey;
     padding: 20px;
     border-radius: 20px;
   }
   article {
     position: relative;
     color:yellow;
     background: darkgray;
     padding: 25px;
   }
   input {
     width: 80px;
     height: 35px;
     font-size: 120%;
   }
 </style>
 <body>

   <h1>Web Worker: The highest prime number</h1>
   <article>The prime numbers:
     <output id="result"></output>
     <div id="status"></div>
   </article>
   <div id="actions">
     <input type="text" name="upto" id="upto"/>
     <button onclick="start()" title="Start the work">Start</button>
     <button onclick="stop()" title="Stop the work and go have a drink">Stop</button>
   </div>
   <script>
     var myWorker;
```

```
    function start() {
      console.log("WebWorker: Starting");
      myWorker = new Worker("highPrime2.js");
      myWorker.addEventListener("message", primeHandler, false);
      var maxNum = $('#upto').val();
      myWorker.postMessage({'cmd': 'start', 'upto': maxNum});
    }

    function stop() {
      if (myWorker) {
        var msg = "<br/>WebWorker: Terminating " + new Date();
        console.log(msg);
        $('#status').append(msg);
        myWorker.terminate();
        myWorker = null;
      }
    }
    function primeHandler(event) {
      console.log ('got e:'+event.data);
      if (is_numeric(event.data)) {
        $('#result').append(event.data);
      }
      else {
        $('#status').append(JSON.stringify(event.data) );
      }
    }

    function is_numeric(input){
      return typeof(input)=='number';
    }
  </script>

</body>
</html>
```

Example 3-4. highPrime2.js, the more controllable Web Worker

```
<script>
//
// A simple way to find prime numbers
// Please note the self refers to the Worker context inside the Worker.
 self.addEventListener('message', function(e) {
   var data = e.data;
   var shouldRun = true;

   switch (data.cmd) {
     case 'stop':
       postMessage('Worker stopped the prime calculation (Al Gore is happy now) ' +
         data.msg );
       shouldRun = false;
       self.close(); // Terminates the Worker.
       break;
     case 'start':
      postMessage("Worker start working upto: " + data.upto + " (" + new Date()+ ")<br/>");
       var numbers = isPrime(data.upto);
       postMessage("Got back these numbers: "+ numbers + "<br/>");
```

```
        break;
      default:
        postMessage('Dude, unknown cmd: ' + data.msg);
    };
  }, false);

  // simple calculation of primes (not the most efficient - but works)
  function isPrime(number) {
    var numArray = "";
    var thisNumber;
    var divisor;
    var notPrime;
    var thisNumber = 3;
    while(thisNumber < number) {
      var divisor = parseInt( thisNumber / 2);
      var notPrime = 0;
      while(divisor > 1) {
        if(thisNumber % divisor == 0) {
          notPrime = 1;
          divisor = 0;
        }
        else {
          divisor = divisor - 1;
        }
      }
      if(notPrime == 0) {
        numArray += (thisNumber + " ");
      }
      thisNumber = thisNumber + 1;
    }
    return numArray;
  }
</script>
```

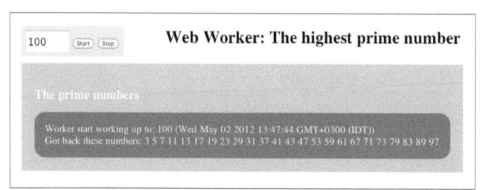

Figure 3-2. Prime number calculation in progress

Parsing Data with Workers

Web Workers are great for handling long-running tasks. In modern web applications, there are many cases in which we need to handle large amounts of data. If you have a large JSON string you wish to parse and it will take ~250 milliseconds (or more), you should use Web Workers. This way, your users will love you and won't hate the fact that the web app doesn't feel responsive.

The following example shows how you can use a simple Web Worker to parse this string and get a nice JSON object you can work with in return.

Example 3-5. Code in Main-web-app-page.html that works with a returned JSON object

```
var worker = new Worker("worker-parser.js");

//when the data is fetched (e.g. in our xhr) -> this event handler
//is called to action
worker.onmessage = function(event){
    //let's get our JSON structure back
    var jsonObj = event.data;

    //work with the JSON object
    showData(jsonObj);
};

//send the 'huge' JSON string to parse
worker.postMessage(jsonText);
```

Example 3-6. worker-parser.js, a Web Worker that handles the actual JSON processing

```
self.onmessage = function(event){

    //the JSON string comes in as event.data
    var jsonText = event.data;

    //parse the structure
    var jsonObj = JSON.parse(jsonText);

    //send back to the JSON obj.
    self.postMessage(jsonObj);
};
```

Transferable Objects

In Firefox and Chrome (since version 13), we have the option to send `ArrayBuffer`s to and from a Web Worker using an algorithm called structured cloning[1]. The option to use `postMessage()` not just for strings, but complex types like `File`, `Blob`, `ArrayBuffer`, and JSON objects, makes this an important enhancement. Structured cloning is a

---

1. *https://developer.mozilla.org/en/DOM/The_structured_clone_algorithm*

powerful algorithm for any web developer, but it's still a copy operation that can take hundreds of milliseconds.

Chrome 17+ offers another performance boost through a new message-passing approach called *Transferable Objects.* This implementation makes sure that the data is transferred and not copied from one context to another. It is a "move" operation and not a copy, which vastly improves the performance of sending data to a Worker. It's similar to a pass-by-reference operation that we have in other languages. In a "normal" pass-by-reference we will have the same pointer to the data; however, here the "version" from the calling context is no longer available once the object is transferred to the new context. In other words, when we transfer an `ArrayBuffer` from our main web app page to the Web Worker, the original `ArrayBuffer` is cleared and we can no longer access it. Instead, its contents are transferred to the Worker context and are accessible only in the Web Worker's scope.

There is a new (prefixed) version of `postMessage()` in Chrome 17+ that supports transferable objects. It takes two arguments, the `ArrayBuffer` message and a list of items that should be transferred:

```
worker.webkitPostMessage(arrayBuffer, [arrayBuffer]);
```

You can also send messages through the window object. This approach requires adding the `targetOrigin` because we can post this message to different workers.

```
window.webkitPostMessage(arrayBuffer, targetOrigin, [arrayBuffer]);
```

These approaches allow massive data manipulation, image processing, WebGL textures, etc., to be passed between the Web Worker and the main app with less impact on memory footprint and speed.

CHAPTER 4

Inline Workers

There are cases in which you will want to create your Worker script "on the fly" in response to some event that your web app has fired. In other cases, you might want to have a self-contained page without having to create separate Worker files. Sometimes, you might wish to have your entire web app encapsulated in one page: you want to be able to fetch the app with one Ajax call, or bundle it as a Chrome extension. Inline Workers support these use cases.

The example below shows how we can use the new `BlobBuilder`[1] interface to inline your Worker code in the same HTML file.

Example 4-1. Creating an inline Worker with a javascript/worker type

```
<script id="worker1" type="javascript/worker">
// This script won't be parsed by JS engines because its type is JavaScript/worker.
// Simple code to calculate prime number and send it back to the parent page.
    self.onmessage = function(e) {
    self.postMessage("<h3>Worker: Started the calculation</h3><ul>");
      var n = 1;
      search: while (n < 500) {
        n += 1;
        for (var i = 2; i <= Math.sqrt(n); i += 1)
          if (n % i == 0)
            continue search;
        // found a prime!
        postMessage("<li>Worker: Found another prime: " + n + "</li>");
      }
      postMessage("</ul><h3>Worker: Done</h3>");
    }
</script>
```

You can see that we are using *javascript/worker* in the type so the JavaScript engine won't parse this code (yet). Next, we calculate the prime numbers up to 500 and send messages to the parent page after each prime is found.

---

1. *http://dev.w3.org/2009/dap/file-system/file-writer.html#the-blobbuilder-interface*

In the main page, we will create a BlobBuilder with the code we have under the script Id "worker1." Then, by using window.URL.createObjectURL we will create a new File (or Blob) that represents our data. Firefox and Chrome both have the ability to use win dow.URL; however, in Chrome/Safari/other WebKit browsers, we will use window.web kitURL.

Example 4-2. Creating a Worker using BlobBuilder

```
<script>
    // Creating the BlobBuilder and adding our Web Worker code to it.
    var bb = new (window.BlobBuilder || window.WebKitBlobBuilder ||
                window.MozBlobBuilder)();
    bb.append(document.querySelector('#worker1').textContent);

    // Creates a simple URL string which can be used to reference
    // data stored in a DOM File / Blob object.
    // In Chrome, there's a nice page to view all of the created
    // blob URLs: chrome://blob-internals/

    // OurUrl enable our code to run in Chrome and Firefox.
    var ourUrl = window.webkitURL || window.URL;
    var worker = new Worker(ourUrl.createObjectURL(bb.getBlob()));

    worker.onmessage = function(e) {
      status(e.data);
    }
    worker.postMessage();
</script>
```

Example 4-3 includes the HTML page with some elements that show what goes on while the Web Worker is finding prime numbers. The main disadvantage to this technique is that it will be harder to debug your Web Worker JavaScript code. One way to be more productive would be to test your Web Worker as an external file. Then, only after you are happy with the results, put it back in the page as an inline Web Worker.

Web Worker: Inline worker example

This is an example for inline worker that we creating 'on the fly' without the need to fetch our JavaScript code of the worker from another file.
It is useful method to create a self-contained page without having to create separate worker file.
With the new BlobBuilder interface, you can "inline" your worker in the same HTML file as your main logic by creating a BlobBuilder and appending the worker code as a string.

- Worker: Found another prime: 379
- Worker: Found another prime: 383
- Worker: Found another prime: 389
- Worker: Found another prime: 397
- Worker: Found another prime: 401
- Worker: Found another prime: 409
- Worker: Found another prime: 419
- Worker: Found another prime: 421
- Worker: Found another prime: 431
- Worker: Found another prime: 433
- Worker: Found another prime: 439
- Worker: Found another prime: 443
- Worker: Found another prime: 449
- Worker: Found another prime: 457
- Worker: Found another prime: 461
- Worker: Found another prime: 463
- Worker: Found another prime: 467
- Worker: Found another prime: 479
- Worker: Found another prime: 487
- Worker: Found another prime: 491
- Worker: Found another prime: 499

Worker: Done

Figure 4-1. Results of the inline Worker hunting for prime numbers

Example 4-3. Inline Web Worker

```
<!DOCTYPE html>
<html>
  <head>
    <meta charset="utf-8" />
    <title>Web Worker: Inline Worker example</title>
    <meta name="author" content="Ido Green">
    <script src="http://ajax.googleapis.com/ajax/libs/jquery/1/jquery.min.js"></script>
  </head>

  <style>
    #status {
      background: lightGreen;
      border-radius: 15px;
      padding: 15px;
      overflow: auto;
```

```
    height:450px;
  }
  article {
    background: lightsalmon;
    border-radius: 15px;
    padding: 15px;
    margin-bottom: 15px;
  }
</style>

<body>
  <h1>Web Worker: Inline Worker example</h1>

  <article>
    This is an example for inline Worker that we created "on the fly" without the need
to fetch our JavaScript code of the Worker from another file.<br/>
    It is a useful method to create a self-contained page without having to create a
separate Worker file.<br/>
    With the new BlobBuilder interface, you can "inline" your Worker in the same HTML
file as your main logic by creating a BlobBuilder and appending the Worker code as a string.
  </article>

  <div id="status"></div>

  <script id="worker1" type="JavaScript/worker">
    // This script won't be parsed by JS engines because its type is JavaScript/worker.
    // We have here some simple code to calculate prime numbers and send them back to the
parent page.
    self.onmessage = function(e) {
    self.postMessage("<h3>Worker: Started the calculation</h3><ul>");
      var n = 1;
      search: while (n < 500) {
        n += 1;
        for (var i = 2; i <= Math.sqrt(n); i += 1)
          if (n % i == 0)
            continue search;
        // found a prime!
        postMessage("<li>Worker: Found another prime: " + n + "</li>");
      }
      postMessage("</ul><h3>Worker: Done</h3>");
    }
  </script>

  <script>
    function status(msg) {
      $("#status").append(msg);
    }

    // Creating the BlobBuilder and adding our Web Worker code to it.
    //new BlobBuilder();
    var bb = new (window.BlobBuilder || window.WebKitBlobBuilder)();
    bb.append(document.querySelector('#worker1').textContent);

    // creates a simple URL string that can be used to reference
    // data stored in a DOM File / Blob object.
```

```
      // In Chrome, there's a nice page to view all of the
      // created blob URLs: chrome://blob-internals/
      var worker = new Worker(window.webkitURL.createObjectURL(bb.getBlob()));
      worker.onmessage = function(e) {
        // pass the information we received from the worker and print it
        status(e.data);
      }
      worker.postMessage(); // Start the worker.
    </script>
  </body>
</html>
```

CHAPTER 5

Shared Workers

Shared Web Workers allow multiple web application instances to communicate with a single instance of a shared Worker. Shared Web Workers will be identified by the name or the URL that you provide in their constructor. You instantiate them by creating a new SharedWorker.

One way to leverage shared workers in your web application is by using a single shared Worker as a central point of communication with a server. Multiple Workers can be opened and all view the same picture through the shared Worker. Instead of directly communicating with your servers, the web app will communicate with a shared Worker that buffers changes locally and communicates with the server when online.

The shared worker can also use HTML5 offline capabilities[1] to persist the state of the data and communicate it to the server, based on your web application logic. It's a long-lived task that gives your application the option of persisting data between all open windows and tabs. It also allows your Model (as in the Model-View-Controller design pattern[2]) to be elegantly encapsulated in one central place.

Other good uses for shared Workers include the following:

- Providing a single source of truth for any type of logic that your app needs in more then one place (e.g., user identification, connection status, etc.).
- Ensuring data consistency between windows of the same web app.
- Reducing the memory consumption of multiple web app tabs/windows, by allowing some code (e.g., server communications) to be centralized in one place.

The main event that the shared Web Worker will execute when a client thread connects to it is connect. Each client connection has a port assigned to uniquely identify that

---

1. Currently only FileAPI and WebSQL are supported from Web Workers. However, because IndexedDB is going to replace WebSQL I hope we will see support for it soon.

2. MVC - *http://en.wikipedia.org/wiki/Model%E2%80%93view%E2%80%93controller*

connection. The post-message method and message events get pushed to the port so that the messaging is performed at the connection level.

 Shared Web Workers can also load additional scripts using `import Scripts()`, attach error handlers, and end further communication on a port with `port.close()`.

The Shared Web Worker in Example 5-1 and Example 5-2 counts the number of connections and sends this data back to our web app rendering thread. You can test it by opening several tabs in your browsers from the same domain.

Example 5-1. SharedWorker1.html

```
<!DOCTYPE HTML>
<html>
 <head>
   <meta charset="utf-8" />
   <title>Shared Web Workers: Basic Example</title>
 </head>
 <body>
   <h1>Shared Web Workers: Basic Example</h1>
   <article>
     To create a shared Web Worker, you pass a JavaScript file name to a new instance of
the SharedWorker object:
     <br/>var worker = new SharedWorker("jsworker.js");
     <br/>
     Our web shared Web Worker will count the connection and return the data back to our
listener in this page. You might want to open the Chrome DevTools to see the process.
     <output id="result"></output>
   </article>
   <script>
     var worker = new SharedWorker('sharedWorker1.js');

     worker.port.addEventListener("message", function(e) {
       document.getElementById('result').textContent += " | " + e.data;
     }, false);

     worker.port.start();

     // post a message to the shared Web Worker
     console.log("Calling the worker from script section 1");
     worker.port.postMessage("script-1");
   </script>

   <script>
     // This new script block might be found on a separate tab/window
     // of our web app. Here it's just for the example on the same page.
     console.log("Calling the worker from script section 2");
     worker.port.postMessage("script-2");
   </script>
 </body>
</html>
```

Example 5-2. sharedWorker1.js

```javascript
// This is the code for: 'sharedWorker1.js' file
// Shared workers that handle the connections and Welcome each new script

var connections = 0; // count active connections
self.addEventListener("connect", function(e) {
    var port = e.ports[0];
    connections++;
    port.addEventListener("message", function(e) {
        port.postMessage("Welcome to " + e.data +
            " (On port #" + connections + ")");
    }, false);
    //
    port.start();
}, false);
```

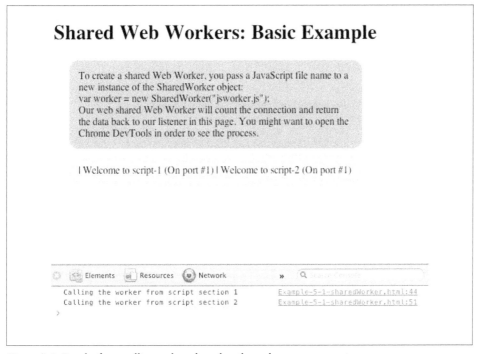

Figure 5-1. Results from calling a shared worker through a common port

In Figure 5-1 you can see the process of calling our shared Web Worker from one \<script> and then calling it again from another \<script> (which could be in a different browser window/tab). The first step is creating the shared Web Worker using its constructor:

```javascript
var worker = new SharedWorker('Example-5-2-sharedWorker.js');
```

Then we add a listener so we could act on the messages that the shared worker sends back:

```
worker.port.addEventListener("message", function(e) {
    document.getElementById('result').textContent += " | " + e.data;
}, false);
```

And now we start the shared Worker:

```
worker.port.start();
```

From now on we can call it using *postMessage:*

```
worker.port.postMessage("our message data");
```

Example 5-3 and Example 5-5 show a more detailed example that shows how to handle connections (in our case, from Twitter) using a shared Worker as the main connector to the Twitter API. It is more efficient in cases in which we think a user might open a few instances of our web app (e.g., a mail client).

Example 5-3. SharedWorkers2.html

```html
<!DOCTYPE HTML>
<html>
  <head>
    <meta charset="utf-8" />
    <meta http-equiv="X-UA-Compatible" content="IE=edge,chrome=1">
    <title>Shared Web Workers: Twitter Example</title>
    <meta name="author" content="Ido Green">
    <script src="http://ajax.googleapis.com/ajax/libs/jquery/1/jquery.min.js"></script>
    <style>
      #result {
        background: lightblue;
        padding: 20px;
        border-radius: 18px;
      }
      #tweets {
        background: yellow;
        border-radius: 28px;
        padding: 20px;
      }
    </style>
  </head>
  <body>

    <h1>Shared Web Workers: Twitter Example</h1>
    <nav>
      <button id="start-button">Start The Shared Worker</button>
      <button id="stop-button">Stop The Shared Worker</button>
    </nav>
    <article>In this example we use a Shared Worker to read tweets and then send them to
the main UI thread. <br/>You will see the messages that we gett from the SharedWorker and
then the tweets for @greenido (yep, that's my username on Twitter)<br/>
    Let's have a look how it's working internally by opening Chrome DevTool on the Console
tab.
    <br/>
```

```html
    <div id="result"></div>
    <div id="tweets"></div>
</article>

<iframe style="width:90%; height: 600px; background: lightgray;"
        src="Example-5-3-b-sharedWorkerTweet.html"></iframe>>

<script>
  var worker;

  function startWorker() {
    console.log("WebWorker: Starting");
    worker = new SharedWorker("sharedWorker2.js");
    worker.port.addEventListener("message", function(e) {
      var curTime = new Date();
      // here we will show the messages between our page and the shared Worker
      $('#result').append( curTime + " ) " + e.data + "<br/>");
      var source = e.data[0].source;
      // in case we have some data from Twitter - let's show it to the user
      if (typeof source != 'undefined' ) {
        var tweets = document.createElement("ul");
        for (var i=0; i < 10; i++) {
          if (typeof e.data[i] != 'undefined' &&
                e.data[i].text != 'undefined') {
            var tweetTextItem = document.createElement("li");
            var tweetText = document.createTextNode(e.data[i].text + " | " +
                e.data[i].source  + " (" +
                e.data[i].created_at + ")" ) ;
            tweetTextItem.appendChild(tweetText);
            tweets.appendChild(tweetTextItem);
          }
          // update the DOM outside our loop so it will be efficient action
          console.log("WebWorker: Updated the DOM with Tweets");
          $("#tweets").append(tweets);
        }

        // just to help us analyze what we got as data form the shared Worker
        console.log ("msg we got back: "+ JSON.stringify(e));
      }, false);
    worker.onerror = function(e){
      throw new Error(e.message + " (" + e.filename + ":" + e.lineno + ")");
    };

    worker.port.start();
    // post a message to the shared Web Worker
    console.log("Calling the worker with @greenido as user");
    worker.port.postMessage({
      cmd: "start",
      user: "greenido"});
  }

  function stopWorker() {
    if (worker != undefined) {
      worker.port.postMessage({ cmd: "stop" });
      console.log("WebWorker: Stop the party");
```

```
          // You might use worker = null if you wish not to use the Worker from now
        }
      }

      // when the DOM is ready - attached our 2 actions to the buttons
      $(function() {
        $('#start-button').click(function() {
          startWorker();
        });
        $('#stop-button').click(function() {
          stopWorker();
        });
      });

    </script>
  </body>
</html>
```

Example 5-4. inner iframe we use in SharedWorkers2.html

```
<!DOCTYPE HTML>
<html>
  <head>
    <meta charset="utf-8" />
    <meta http-equiv="X-UA-Compatible" content="IE=edge,chrome=1">
    <title>Shared Web Workers: Twitter Example</title>
    <meta name="author" content="Ido Green">
    <script src="http://ajax.googleapis.com/ajax/libs/jquery/1/jquery.min.js"></script>
    <style>
      #result {
        background: orange;
        padding: 20px;
        border-radius: 18px;
      }
      #tweets {
        background: grey;
        border-radius: 28px;
        padding: 20px;
      }
    </style>
  </head>
  <body>

    <h1>Shared Web Workers: inner iframe</h1>
    <nav>
      <button id="start-button">Start The Shared Worker</button>
      <button id="stop-button">Stop The Shared Worker</button>
    </nav>
    <article>
      Inner iframe that in the real world could be another tab/window of our web app.
      <div id="result"></div>
      <div id="tweets"></div>
    </article>
    <script>
      var worker;
```

```
function startWorker() {
  console.log("WebWorker: Starting");
  worker = new SharedWorker("Example-5-4-sharedWorkerTweet.js");
  worker.port.addEventListener("message", function(e) {
    var curTime = new Date();
    // here we will show the messages between our page and the shared Worker
    $('#result').append( curTime + " ) " + e.data + "<br/>");
    var source = e.data[0].source;
    // in case we have some data from Twitter - let's show it to the user
    if (typeof source != 'undefined' ) {
      var tweets = document.createElement("ul");
      for (var i=0; i < 10; i++) {
       if (typeof e.data[i] != 'undefined' &&
             e.data[i].text != 'undefined') {
          var tweetTextItem = document.createElement("li");
          var tweetText = document.createTextNode(e.data[i].text + " | " +
            e.data[i].source  + " (" +
            e.data[i].created_at + ")" ) ;
          tweetTextItem.appendChild(tweetText);
          tweets.appendChild(tweetTextItem);
       }
      }
      // update the DOM outside our loop so it will be efficient action
      console.log("WebWorker: Updated the DOM with Tweets");
      $("#tweets").append(tweets);

    }
  }, false);
  worker.onerror = function(e){
    throw new Error(e.message + " (" + e.filename + ":" + e.lineno + ")");
  };

  worker.port.start();
  // post a message to the shared Web Worker
  console.log("Calling the worker with @greenido as user");
  worker.port.postMessage({
    cmd: "start",
    user: "greenido"});
}

function stopWorker() {
  if (worker != undefined) {
    worker.port.postMessage({ cmd: "stop" });
    console.log("WebWorker: Stop the party");
    // You might use worker = null if you wish not to use the Worker from now
  }
}

// when the DOM is ready - attached our 2 actions to the buttons
$(function() {
  $('#start-button').click(function() {
    startWorker();
  });
  $('#stop-button').click(function() {
    stopWorker();
```

```
      });
    });

  </script>
 </body>
</html>
```

Example 5-5. sharedWorker2.js

```javascript
//
// Shared workers that handle the connections and Welcome each new script
// @author Ido Green
// @date   11/11/2011
var connections = 0;  // count active connections
var updateDelay = 60000; // = 1min delay
var port;
var user;

function getURL(user) {
  return 'http://twitter.com/statuses/user_timeline/' + user
  + '.json?count=' + 12 + '&callback=processTweets';
}

function readTweets() {
  try {
    var url = getURL(user);
    port.postMessage("Worker: Attempting To Read Tweets for user - " + user +
      " from: "+ url);
    importScripts(url);
  }
  catch (e) {
    port.postMessage("Worker: Error - " + e.message);
    setTimeout(readTweets, updateDelay); // lets do it every 2min
  }
}

function processTweets(data) {
  if (data.length > 0) {
    port.postMessage("Worker: New Tweets - " + data.length);
    port.postMessage(data);
  } else {
    port.postMessage("Worker: New Tweets - 0");
  }
  setTimeout(readTweets, updateDelay);
}



//
// The controller that manage the actions/commands/connections
//
self.addEventListener("connect", function (e) {
  port = e.ports[0];
  connections++;
  port.addEventListener("message", function (e) {
    var data = e.data;
```

```
  switch (data.cmd) {
    case 'start':
      port.postMessage("Worker: Starting You are connection number:"+ connections);
      user = data.user;
      readTweets();
      break;
    case 'stop':
      port.postMessage("Worker: Stopping");
      self.close();
      break;
    default:
      port.postMessage("Worker: Error - Unknown Command");
  };

}, false);
port.start();
}, false);
```

Figure 5-2 shows how the Shared Web Worker example will look. The connection to the shared Worker is done first from the main window and then from the iframe (that mimics the case of another instance of the web app in another window or tab).

Shared Web Workers: Twitter Example

(Start The Shared Worker) (Stop The Shared Worker)
In this example we used a Shared Worker in order to read tweets and then send them to the main UI thread.
You will see the messages that we are getting from the SharedWorker and then the tweets for @greenido user (yep, that's my user on Twitter)
Let's have a look how it's working internally by opening Chrome DevTool on the Console tab.

Thu Mar 22 2012 12:16:03 GMT+0200 (IST)) Worker: Starting You are connection number:1
Thu Mar 22 2012 12:16:03 GMT+0200 (IST)) Worker: Attempting To Read Tweets for user - greenido from: http://twitter.com/statuses/user_timeline/greenido.json?
count=12&callback=processTweets
Thu Mar 22 2012 12:16:03 GMT+0200 (IST)) Worker: New Tweets - 9
Thu Mar 22 2012 12:16:03 GMT+0200 (IST)) [object Object],[object Object],[object Object],[object Object],[object Object],[object Object],[object Object],[object Object],[object Object]

- Save yourself some hours of debugging your web app with: http://t.co/F396BVR3 #HTML5 I <a href="http://itunes.apple.com/us/app/twitter/id409789998?mt=12" rel="nofollow">Twitter for Mac</a> (Thu Mar 22 08:00:16 +0000 2012)
- Asynchronous UIs - the future of web user interfaces http://t.co/1uXRTJuI thx to @maccman I <a href="http://twitter.com/tweetbutton" rel="nofollow">Tweet Button</a> (Thu Mar 22 06:47:37 +0000 2012)
- @freddy33 Now you are an official 'Aars katan'... :) I <a href="http://itunes.apple.com/us/app/twitter/id409789998?mt=12" rel="nofollow">Twitter for Mac</a> (Wed Mar 21 08:13:58 +0000 2012)
- "@peterlubbers: http://t.co/rQopJ1Yn is down, pretty cool 404 page though. http://t.co/QVtGezs3" - is it Paris that did it? I <a href="http://itunes.apple.com/us/app/twitter/id409789998?mt=12" rel="nofollow">Twitter for Mac</a> (Tue Mar 20 18:29:01 +0000 2012)
- Good post that summarize 25 Chrome Dev Tools 'secrets' that will make you more productive: http://t.co/Hqtfk0Fz I <a href="http://itunes.apple.com/us/app/twitter/id409789998?mt=12" rel="nofollow">Twitter for Mac</a> (Sun Mar 18 07:29:52 +0000 2012)
- @mahemoff Agree with every word... soon I hope to have something cool for you :) I web (Sat Mar 17 20:28:50 +0000 2012)
- @freakonomics @WNYC only if you know the price before you try it! :) I web (Sat Mar 17 19:44:57 +0000 2012)
- Cake http://t.co/1WsCZczH I <a href="http://instagr.am" rel="nofollow">Instagram</a> (Fri Mar 16 11:16:35 +0000 2012)
- Cupcakes http://t.co/S5qVNjCe I <a href="http://instagr.am" rel="nofollow">Instagram</a> (Fri Mar 16 11:13:14 +0000 2012)

Shared Web Workers: inner iframe

(Start The Shared Worker) (Stop The Shared Worker)
Inner iframe that in the real world could be another tab/window of our web app.

Thu Mar 22 2012 12:16:05 GMT+0200 (IST)) Worker: Starting You are connection number:2
Thu Mar 22 2012 12:16:05 GMT+0200 (IST)) Worker: Attempting To Read Tweets for user - greenido from:
http://twitter.com/statuses/user_timeline/greenido.json?count=12&callback=processTweets
Thu Mar 22 2012 12:16:05 GMT+0200 (IST)) Worker: New Tweets - 9
Thu Mar 22 2012 12:16:05 GMT+0200 (IST)) [object Object],[object Object],[object Object],[object Object],[object Object],[object Object],[object Object],[object Object],[object Object]

- Save yourself some hours of debugging your web app with: http://t.co/F396BVR3 #HTML5 I <a href="http://itunes.apple.com/us/app/twitter/id409789998?mt=12" rel="nofollow">Twitter for Mac</a> (Thu Mar 22 08:00:16 +0000 2012)
- Asynchronous UIs - the future of web user interfaces http://t.co/1uXRTJuI thx to @maccman I <a href="http://twitter.com/tweetbutton" rel="nofollow">Tweet Button</a> (Thu Mar 22 06:47:37 +0000 2012)

Figure 5-2. Shared workers running across iframes

CHAPTER 6

Debug Your Workers

Because Web Workers JavaScript files aren't part of the files you will find in Firefox's firebug or in Safari's web inspector, it will be difficult to debug them. These script files aren't part of the current page scope, and the browser won't show them to us. Luckily, in Chrome (15+) we have a great option to debug Web Workers in the Chrome Dev Tools. We will see how to use this tool later in this chapter.

If you aren't using Chrome, there is an option to gain information when an error occurs. The Web Workers specification[1] shows us that an error event (`onerror` handler) should be fired when a runtime script error occurs in a Worker. The main properties in the `onerror` handler are the following:

message
> The error message itself.

lineno
> The number of the line inside our Web Worker that caused the error.

filename
> The name of the file inside the Worker in which the error occurred.

That should be all the information you need to be able to fix your "errors," right?

You can override the `onerror` function with a version that will throw an error with enough information to help us see what's happening inside the Worker. You may also add some other parameters that are specific to your case. For example, if your Worker is handling connections, you can add their data (e.g., number of open connections, number of ideal connections, etc.) to this error message. This is a simple way to understand where your code is broken.

```
var worker = new Worker("worker.js");
worker.onerror = function(e){
 throw new Error(e.message + " (" + e.filename + ":" + e.lineno + ")" );
};
```

---

1. *http://www.w3.org/TR/workers/*

Debugging in Chrome Dev Tools

Chrome (15+) facilitates debugging of Web Workers by injecting fake Workers implementations. These injections simulate Web Workers using an `iframe` within a Worker's client page. This is a powerful tool that lets us debug workers in a much more productive way. To get the new Chrome Dev Tool console, you will need to navigate to the scripts pane in Dev Tools. Check the *Debug* checkbox to the right of Worker inspectors, and then reload the page. The Web Worker script will show up under Worker inspectors, as shown in Figure 6-1.

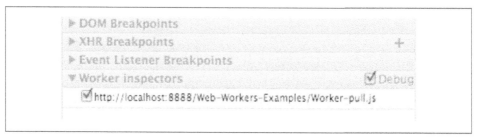

Figure 6-1. Worker inspectors in Chrome Dev Tools

In Chrome 17+ you will see the new UI shown in Figure 6-2.

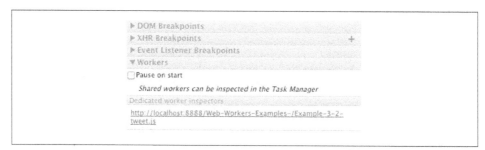

Figure 6-2. Workers in Chrome 17+

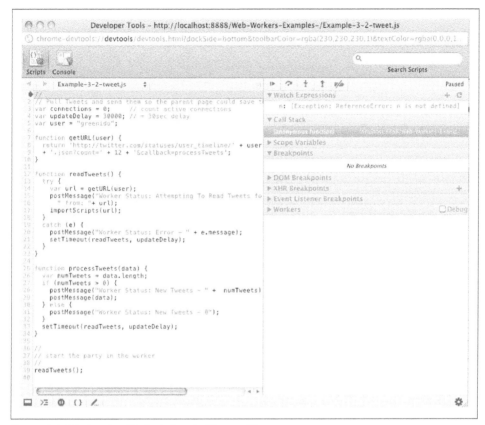

Figure 6-3. Worker Dev Tool window in Chrome 17+

Chrome 17+ offers the ability to debug your shared Workers, as shown in Figure 6-3. Open the task manager, and between all the tasks (=open tabs and other process) you will see one for the shared Worker. Click on it and you will get the option to "investigate." This will open a new window with the Chrome Dev Tool.

CHAPTER 7

Web Workers Beyond the Browser: Node

The main motivation to implement Web Workers for NodeJS is to have a set of standard platform-independent concurrency APIs outside the browser. One powerful example is Peter Griess' *node-webworker* module[1], and you can find others on GitHub[2].

These implementations let front-end web developers carry their knowledge of Web Workers technology beyond the browser. They also let developers avoid the NodeJS primitives for managing processes. The `child_process`[3] provides a great deal of functionality, but is easily misinterpreted by developers who have not developed for a UNIX platform. The error reporting APIs in the Web Workers are also more full-featured and verbose than the one provided natively by `child_process`.

Using this module effectively requires understanding that Web Worker instances are relatively heavyweight and should be long-lived. Launching a Worker and maintaining its state requires a high per-instance memory cost. Therefore, it's more efficient to pass messages to existing Workers to create tasks rather than creating a new Web Worker for each work item.

Processes

In the *node-webworker* module each worker implements in its own node process. This is done so we won't need a separate thread (and V8 context) in the main node process. Each node process will be self-contained.

The main advantage of this approach include the following:

---

1. Thanks to Peter Griess and his important work on GitHub (*https://github.com/pgriess/node-webworker*). You can read more in his blog: *http://blog.std.in/2010/07/08/nodejs-webworker-design/*

2. *https://github.com/cramforce/node-worker*

3. *http://www.linux-tutorial.info/modules.php?name=MContent&pageid=83*

Performance

> Modern operating systems are more likely to schedule different processes on different CPUs. This might not always happen for multiple threads within the same process, and with today's multicore processors it make sense to leverage them as we can.

Fault isolation

> If the Worker runs out of memory or triggers an error, it will not cause glitches to other Workers.

Avoiding complexity

> There is no need for a complicated managing layer that observes event loops in a single process.

Each worker is launched by *lib/webworker-child.js*, which is passed to the UNIX socket to be used as a message channel with the parent process. You then can use a web socket in the parent process to pass messages on this channel:

```
new WebSocket('ws+unix://' + sockPath);
```

This script is passed to node as the entry point for the process and is responsible for constructing a V8 script context populated with Web Workers API syntax (e.g., the `postMessage()`, `close()` etc.). All of this action occurs in a context that is separate from the one in which the Worker application will be executing. In this case, each Worker gets a clean Node runtime with the Web Worker API. The Worker application doesn't need to initialize or `require()` any additional libraries or scripts.

Communications

The Web Workers spec describes a message passing API.[4] The Node-based master process will create a dedicated UNIX domain socket per worker. This has much less overhead than TCP, and it allows us to enjoy some UNIX goodies like file descriptor passing. This socket's path will be composed from */tmp/node-webworker-<pid>/<worker-id>*.

<pid>

> PID of the process doing the creating.

<worker-id>

> ID of the worker being created.

---

4. *http://www.whatwg.org/specs/web-apps/current-work/multipage/workers.html#communicating-with-a-dedicated-worker*

Message Format

The messages themselves are in JSON. As with Web Workers in the browser, you should use `JSON.stringify()` and `JSON.parse()` to encode and decode these objects. As a good practice it's suggested to use an object that will encapsulate a message from this format: `{ <type>, <object> }`. This simple protocol allows us to act in the Web Worker on the data (which is passed inside our `<object>` base on the `<type>` we wish). For example, a type could be start, stop, analyze, debug, etc.

Code

Example 7-1 starts a Worker that calculates routes (e.g., the famous problem of finding the best route from L.A. to San Francisco). The code in *main.js* is a generic setup to create the Worker and listen to its output, whereas in the Worker itself we calculate the routes and post the results back.

Example 7-1. main.js

```
var sys = require('sys');
// fetching node-webworker
var Worker = require('webworker');

// create a new worker to calculate routes
var w = new Worker('routes-worker.js');

// listen to messages from the Worker and in our case kill it when we get the first message
(with or without the calculated route
w.onmessage = function(e) {
    sys.debug('* Got mesage: ' + sys.inspect(e));
    w.terminate();
};

// ask the Worker to run on a 'test' route from L.A. to San Francisco
w.postMessage({ route : 'lax-sfo' });
```

Example 7-2. routes-worker.js

```
onmessage = function(data) {
    // calculating the route here
    // ...
    postMessage({ route : 'json obj with the route details' });
};

onclose = function() {
    sys.debug('route-worker shutting down.');
};
```

API

The supported standard Web Worker API methods include the following:

`postMessage(e)`

> In both workers and the parent.

`onmessage(e)`

> In both workers and the parent.

`onerror(e)`

> In both workers and the parent.

`terminate()`

> In the parent. You don't need it in the Web Worker, as it will finish on its own.

Additional Resources

- All of this book's example code can be found on GitHub: *https://github.com/green ido/Web-Workers-Examples-*
- Specifications: *http://www.whatwg.org/specs/web-workers/current-work/*
- Mozilla Developer Network: *https://developer.mozilla.org/en/Using_web_workers*
- The basics of Web Workers: *http://www.html5rocks.com/en/tutorials/workers/ba sics/*
- Live example of Web Workers that find routes on a map: *http://slides.html5rocks .com/#web-workers*
- Live example I've written using Web Workers to calculate prime numbers while you can control them (start/stop) using commands: *http://ido-green.appspot.com/ examples/webWorkers/highPrime2.html*
- Canvas & Web Workers demo: This app uses canvas to draw out a scene. You'll see that when you use Web Workers this scene is drawn in pieces; this is done by telling the Web Worker to compute a slice of pixels. The Web Worker itself cannot manipulate the canvas because of the restrictions it has. It will therefore pass the computed information back to the main page and the drawing will be done from this page: *http://nerget.com/rayjs-mt/rayjs.html*.

About the Author

Ido is a Developer Advocate for Google Chrome OS. He has been a developer and building companies for more then 15 years. He still likes to develop web applications, but only ones with amazing UX. He has a wide array of skills and experience, including Java, php, perl, JavaScript--and all aspects of agile development and scaling systems.

Get even more for your money.

Join the O'Reilly Community, and register the O'Reilly books you own. It's free, and you'll get:

- $4.99 ebook upgrade offer
- 40% upgrade offer on O'Reilly print books
- Membership discounts on books and events
- Free lifetime updates to ebooks and videos
- Multiple ebook formats, DRM FREE
- Participation in the O'Reilly community
- Newsletters
- Account management
- 100% Satisfaction Guarantee

Signing up is easy:

1. Go to: oreilly.com/go/register
2. Create an O'Reilly login.
3. Provide your address.
4. Register your books.

Note: English-language books only

To order books online:
oreilly.com/store

For questions about products or an order:
orders@oreilly.com

To sign up to get topic-specific email announcements and/or news about upcoming books, conferences, special offers, and new technologies:
elists@oreilly.com

For technical questions about book content:
booktech@oreilly.com

To submit new book proposals to our editors:
proposals@oreilly.com

O'Reilly books are available in multiple DRM-free ebook formats. For more information:
oreilly.com/ebooks

Spreading the knowledge of innovators   oreilly.com

Have it your way.

Ingram Content Group UK Ltd.
Milton Keynes UK
UKHW030615080323
418199UK00007B/370